Kaleidoscope

Kaleidoscope

Poems

Tina Barr

Iris Press
Oak Ridge, Tennessee

Cover Art: "Monarch Kaleidoscope"
Copyright © 2014 by Joyce Black-Woerz

Book Design: Robert B. Cumming, Jr.

Library of Congress Cataloging-in-Publication Data

Barr, Tina, 1955-
  [Poems. Selections]
  Kaleidoscope : poems / Tina Barr.
      pages cm
  ISBN 978-1-60454-230-1 (pbk. : alk. paper)
  I. Title.
  PS3552.A73187A6 2015
  811'.54—dc23
                          2015003545

Acknowledgements

Grateful thanks to the following publications where some of these poems first appeared:

The Annals of Scholarship: "Scope" ("In the Kaleidoscope's Chamber"), "Shiny Brite"

The Antioch Review: "Hour of the Cardinals"

Arts & Letters: "Refuge," "Pilgrim"

boundary 2 (online blog): "In This Neighborhood," "Souvenir," "The Tear of Fire," "Our Cleaning Lady's Son" ("The Cleaning Lady's Son")

Brilliant Corners: "Blue Rose," "Blue Fawn"

Chapter 16 (online): "Golden Moon Casino"

The Chattahoochee Review: "Morphic Fields"

Crab Orchard Review: "Thieves"

Hotel Amerika: "Jailbait," "Beauty"

Kakalak: "The Raggle Taggle Gypsies"

Limestone: "Dessert," "Sparrow's Vision"

The Mississippi Review: "The Guardians of Chocolate," "The Ecology of *Atlas*"

New South: "Guns Not For Sale"

Notre Dame Review: "Orphanage Wars," "They Attempt to Hide in the Fiddle Cases," "Henry Darger Comes to Lakebottom Park"

Parthenon West: "The Reading Room Deck"

Shenandoah: "Kaleidoscope of Saints"

Witness: "Before the Prophet's Birthday," "Zabiba," "Lipoma"

Thanks to the Carson McCullers Center for Writers and Musicians, The Ucross Foundation, and the Tennessee Arts Commission. Special thanks to Joyce Black-Woerz, Shara McCallum and Katherine Soniat.

For My Bookends:

Michael Jefry Stevens, composer

&

Daniel T. O'Hara, literary critic

Contents

I

II

III

I

In the Kaleidoscope's Chamber

As I turn the chambered end, the mirrors
seem to stretch the colors as jewels shift,
circling them into wheels of unfolding
flowers; the mind feeds on pattern, incites
us to find it. The chamber fills with purple,
blue bruises, the open jaw of a dead father,
multiplies the tight eyes of liars, orange tubes
of trumpet vine, pink-tipped brushes of mimosa,
filaments sweet as what I concocted in bottles
from a perfume kit as a kid. Green-felt seed pods
of magnolia from which spring tiny hooks like wires,
pine cones, maple burrs. My husband's hands
tab the keys, dicing white and black. My ears
arrange it as music; outside are birds, ushering us in.

Blue Rose

for Sheila Jordan's bebop in Provence

Someone's picked lettuce from sunlight,
brined mussels in vinegar and bruised thyme,
to work against the sweetness of smoked salmon,
snipped the heads and tails of four anchovies,
split grey and white, arranged on a plate.

They taste of a concentration of salt
breaking into the mouth. As if their bodies
are permeated by a sea where vessels of olives
leached their oil into the blue.
Or Tyre's purple, boiled from snails.

Sheila sings as if she has fed off feelings,
her insides transparent. Her voice a fluid.
Like a wound inside my mouth when
a marzipan grape sprayed with color
spurts its brandy.

Blue rings inside me. I am the hood
of a bell slammed by the clapper;
sound shakes
colors and tones. I see my split selves
come back to rest, cast, and whole.

Blue Fawn

for Herb Robertson

Pink mountain lions splay their claws
in the visual cage of a carpet from Herat.
Stylized, they cavort, linked by floral
vining to other medallions that enclose
the deer they hunt.

          Inside the black
box of a nightclub, the band hunts
music that weaves itself through air.
It is invisible, like so much discounted
in the mind's cage.

          But we have ears,
can hear something behind the bass,
thrumming that sets us *towards*,
like a bee who comes into a window,
crawls its softness along my leg,
in a sniff, for something, a trace of soap
maybe, that could be phlox or rose.

But this is not artificial.

They bring the smallest rolling cases
for clothes, the weight that matters is
in instruments: cymbals, tenor sax, a bass
in canvas Joe steers through streets.

My husband cuts his fingers on the piano's teeth.

A blue fawn steps in, paws and feeds,
wades in grassy shapes the notes make,
and is blown aside by what pours open
from the trumpet, growls through Herb's
mute. The panther tacking back and forth.

Herb was riding his bike to try to get
six weeks of owed money from neighbors
on his paper route, who were never home.

He saw a lamp on, swerved, crashed, got
twenty-five stitches so he had to shift
playing to the other side of his mouth.
With a new embouchure a lion came
out of his trumpet.

            He tells me about
his mutes: cup, bubble, tuxedo plunger,
pixie in red, wah-wah, a felt mute like
a yamaka.

The band's recording in Warsaw
and I wander the castle's carpet display
and other museums, watch black and
white films. A woman makes bread
in a big wood tub, wears a kerchief,
scrapes dough from her hands with a spoon.

The Catholics all in dirndls and aprons
for Corpus Christi, Jews hidden the other
side of wheat fields.

Poles dressed out of the Brothers Grimm.

When Hansel and Gretel seek a way out,
birds eat the bread they've left to mark a path.

That's the foolishness of artists,
thinking they can wander into forests
and go home.

No one gets back, except
a blue fawn might appear, if you believe
hard enough, and lead you somewhere.

Shiny Brite

Lost pinecone elves, wearing dunce-cap hats
of flocked paper turn up. Alert inside Ebay,
their eyes look sideways, each blue-eyed,
painted by Japanese not blinded by a light
much brighter than Christmas. The elves stand
on clog-feet of pressed cotton. Chenille
pipe-cleaner arms taper like fitted sleeves,
yellow or bright pink, little velvets. One
holds up a stocking, sitting his cotton body
on a tiny pinecone; a mushroom emerges
from the gold cardboard circle he is glued to.

In factories after the war, we helped the
Japanese recover. In my mother's cold garden,
the inner skin orange, bark peels from oak leaf
hydrangea, shedding itself. In a whoosh
like the flash of gas, their clothes evaporated.
Dangling their hands, in Nagasaki people
sleepwalked home, faces peeling like loquat.
Its dried leaves make a tea, *biwa cha*, said to
beautify. Elves' faces, after the occupation's
heyday, get pinker, as if whoever dyed the plastic
thought reddish complexions best for export.

I wake at night and think of those blinded
by the bomb, and how we blind ourselves,
all those rapes at Okinawa and the pan-pan girls.
My mother changed the subject; her not-love
stung in little verbal clots, like milk in a woman
whose breast burst a white lump the size of a
summer orange from glands plugged with the burning.
Mandarin oranges grew in Kagoshima.
We found them in the toes of Christmas stockings.
My mother fed me segments in syrup from a can
on which a Japanese beauty wore a comb, held a fan.

Dessert

Canned mandarin oranges was one, or fruit cup,
but in the Westbury's dining room horses raced
neck and neck along the walls; a blue mermaid lounged
inside my Shirley Temple, plastic arms hooked back
over the lip of the glass, two cherries magnified, swimming
in ginger ale. My grandmother's voice, high-boned,
drifted in smoke as her legs crossed and uncrossed.
My hands in my velvet lap turned her pearls; I wore
black patent shoes with a button hard to push through.
Waiters flourished lamb chops; frills dressed their bones.
I chose from a cart. Strawberries nestled in yellow cream,
the fluted edge of pastry, crust like a shortbread.
Strawberries glazed under sugar, berries bedded in rows.
My grandmother crossed Park, got hit by a car, and thrown.

Masque

The waist that could draw men's eyes has lost
its elastic. Ovaries flatten on a microscope's
slide, cells pressed on a glass insert to fit
a kaleidoscope.

Turning on fortune's wheel,
we have our time on its climbing. Nights,
children dab their tongues in gelato. Romeos
and Juliets glitter in the storefronts' blaze over cobbles.

Next: falling breasts, the pullet's
chin. A girl and her grandmother share brown
eyes, liquid as rabbits'; true blonde waves will grey,
one face become the other.

Inside my mask,
my husband recognizes my eyes. I memorize his white
eyelashes, as if pigments rubbed to dust, constitute us:
lime, red ochre, lapis, black clay.

In Siena page boys
off the frescos scroll, make figure eights
with ruffling colored banners on poles,
throw them high up, caught as they plummet.

A sky inflates beyond boxed rosemary
that flavors boar stew. In close-set fields
Lorenzetti's prince hunts them centuries before
we were born.

In a frieze we thrust up pikes, flags,
the t-shirts and baseball caps that define some
"us," before the black-hooded one bends his face
to kiss us into the fairy tale from which we never wake.

Kaleidoscope of Saints

Lorenzetti's red bird scoots over
the hands of Francesco d'Assisi,
no it's a tiny carmine angel, its head
set between wings, without a neck.
Transparent, it hovers above the hole
on the back of St. Francis's left palm.
At the saint's deathbed, his donkey wept.

More of those red wings attach
behind Christ's robes, his halo
a gold plate. Beyond him, crowned,
palms upheld, God.
Or are the wings faded fourteenth
century *putti,* whirring like hummingbirds
either side, at hands, feet and shoulders?

Their work, the Hutu called it; Christ's
is to rise. A body gets cold after, as if
refrigerated. What flickered, winged,
votive, shuts down like a monitor, no
load on the chips. A binary mystery,
like this painter's symbols, lost
without my reading of the Bible as manual.

A man's iron rod tumbles wood, stokes
flames he's in charge of; upright red
snakes surround a cauldron big enough
so Cyrinus stands inside it, waist-high in oil,
palms pressed to a steeple. The Hutu hacked
Tutsis with machetes; their madonnas' stomachs
were split watermelons of blood.

And what of San Girolamo's red origami
hat, with its upturned brim?

On the wall behind in a niche, inset,
tilts a pair of scissors.
Its handles' holes are symbolic eyes
through which a god might look.
Is he out of his mind?

Mother

She ate my marrow with a tiny spoon,
the way I dip an avocado from its cup.
Once she'd handed a guest a demitasse
that foamed soap, not rinsed enough.
My father would ask her to hook
the shiny pink balls lowest on the fir.
She'd tuck them so high up, as they fell
they broke open, showed the inner
foil of silver shell. We'd spoon up toast
coated in yolk from chalices of egg cups,
crumbling in salty bacon. Our hamburgers
were grey, our peas burnt. She kept vanilla
fudge swirl in the freezer, because
she had no love to spoon into herself.

II

Outsider artist Henry Darger, a Chicago janitor, created a body of textual, collaged and watercolor work, all discovered in his apartment by his landlords after his death.

I

Henry Darger Comes to Lakebottom Park

In brown faces, five smiles ignite;
behind them a white truck stenciled:
Prison Detail. Like Darger's soldiers,
recruits populate the park, which is, like his
studded with palms, oaks, cypress, pine;
red-hooded, white-bellied, tuxedoed
woodpeckers edge the trees' circumferences.
There are tennis courts, a track, five
diamonds, a house for girl scouts,
a yellow bus pasted under its maples.

Henry Darger filled his parks with girls
and flowers, but his mind upturned scenes
you and I see in dreams. Gardenias send up
their sweet drifts; white skins untwist,
brown in minutes. Magnolias open chalices
of cinnamon. A girl in a blue dress
carries a red basket; red binds her yellow ringlets.
She is his lost sister, given for adoption.
She carries parasols, dolls, pocketbooks;
ribbons change in her hair like rainbows.

At nine he boarded at Catholic school;
at twelve touched himself in public.
At seventeen, escaped the asylum, walked
his own skies to Chicago. He watercolors tiger lilies
tall as trees. Under their pinafores, beneath
smocked, collared, puff-sleeved dresses,

his girls wear genitals like boys. One's torn
dress shows her big-bellied. Others wear only
bonnets and socks; one covers her mouth.
She sees something outside the field of green.

II

Orphanage Wars

Darger's fires look like giant yellow petals.
Magnolia leaves dried to a crisp
crack underfoot, but green-haired girls,
headbands, berets, pigtails in place, run
in pink dresses, some with epaulettes,
through a blue field. Now girls' feet
are bound to stones. Hoisted by their necks,
they're big-eyed as cartoon ducks with tongues.
My own aunts, uncles, cousins,
never saw the fires in our house
behind the yews, even when my brother's
coffin floated, a white boat, trimmed in gilt.

In the den where the enemy Glandelins meet
a girl's face pops through the wall; her hands
pull aside the torn paper. Norma, a girl on horseback,
rides through the pages of Darger's Civil War.
Horse thuds bring up dust. Girls nailed to crosses,
paper dolls with feet torn off, rivulets
of red leak down their chests. Others,
in purple-rimmed cowgirl hats, escape
through fields of slaughtered toddlers.
He names his heroines like trophies. *Jennie,*
Sally, Daisy, Hetty, Violet, Angeline
float yellow-haired in quicksand, cross-eyed.

III

The Tear of Fire

I am a flower girl, wearing
a white skirt stiff with tulle beneath.
A wide pink sash wraps into a bow at my back.
My small hands in white gloves carry a bouquet before me.
Darger's girls hang on long strings, eyes turned back.
Dressed in little black shoes—Thelmas and Ellies.

First orange-red hills, diaphanous,
the substance of mirage. Sheets of fire shake
the way sails luff as they shift in a tack. It starts in our neighbor's attic,
so a fireman climbs a ladder, wearing his face mask, silver tank
on his back. Others axe windows, snake in the hose, climb after it.
The attic blackens. The oak billows like a parachute. Nightmare lives in
    the wood.

IV

They Attempt to Hide in the Fiddle Cases

A girl adorned with ram's horns growing from her head
smiles beneath a rose bush. Zinnias, hollyhock,
delphinium, a butterfly elaborate with eyes
puts its face into each one. Now the girls spin
anemone print dresses; they've slung their legs over stalks,
eye-lashed, pink-mouthed, the tiny noses of kids inked in.
Under pink morning glories a girl hides two valentines.
A few peek naked behind pocketed towers of foxglove.

A man in an Academic cap, missing a tassle,
bares teeth penciled in like five pebbles. The bad
ones wear mustaches and sport doormen's buttons.
He has torn off Jennie's feet and concentrates his hands,
wrists yellow-cuffed, on her neck. His Confederate
soldiers plunge girls to the ground. Many windows bulge
on the house in the distance. In green puffs above
salmon-colored trunks, sparrows speak *sweet, sweet.*

V

Our Cleaning Lady's Son

Pins fell out of her hair; black glasses
made her eyes into a cat's. My sister and I
took her little one into a dirt-floored room
under the yews, persuaded him to pull
down his pants; he stood, beginning to tear.

In Darger's scroll, a little girl wears a boy-scout
tie the color of roses all around her, holds her
hands at her ears, her shorts slid onto her shoes.
Her small penis is drawn in, the way kids
squiggle a hieroglyph in a book's margin.

VI

Jailbait

She has stepped into the body of a rabbit;
she exists on two planes, her face behind
the fence or her face transparent. Darger's
pigtailed blondes jump the mortarboards
of enemy professors, or are they jumping fences?
Cartoon-faced, savage, girls' penises point down.
Beside a pie basket, a pocked, cobbled road
leads to palms and cottages where Jennie Richee
raises sunflowers, trillium, lupine. Glandelins
bayonet a girl in knee socks, her mouth the "o"
of a doughnut. Darger penciled "jump
like cats onto the shoulders of two soldiers."
Forty, six-to-ten-year-olds, line up, shy,
fearful, jubilant, rueful. Their hair cut
as my mother wore hers when dressed
in puffed sleeves, a sailor's collar. Some
girls have no clothes; neither did I, bulleted
with fear, my father calling *comehavesex*.
People overlook the rifles, see meadows fill
with columbine, daffodil, blue swallowtail.
A sparrow grips the water bucket; his beak dips.

VII

The Guardians of Chocolate

Darger's red-haired girls, four brunettes, each
draw the shake up the straw so it melts
on their tongues. One holds her fountain
glass in two hands. Fanny, our maid, ambled,
slim inside the uniform, white against her skin;
dirt scuffed up under our sneakers. Fanny and
I would pass the only farmhouse left, cross
the highway. I'd swivel on the stool. I can hear
the rotor; it spun milk into a cold thickness.
I'd eye the steel canister that held the extra.
The girls wear yellow trousers, red shirts
pocked with yellow buttons, epaulettes; beanies
flag a twist of blue ostrich. My grandmother paid
for a maid, so we weren't alone with her son.

VIII

Beauty

A grey sand track rings Georgia's Lakebottom
Park, every inch printed with dots, waffles,
lozenges, squares distinct as fingerprints.
Each morning the same faces pass, two
round, brown, smiles rising like platters
of warm food carried in my direction.
A tall line of a man, veins wired in his legs,
eyes never drift from wherever he is heading.
Shirtless, skin buffed and chestnut, someone
runs sixty steps up the high school's front.
I name him Proportion, Leonardo's drawing
in a wheel or circle. A woman presses towards me,
scarf tied under her chin, long sleeves, knee socks
even in this heat. *Salaam Aleikum*, I say it.
She raises her hand gently in my direction.

III

Thieves

I look for the crooked "g" in the word
Sirgany, a shop on the corner of Al Muezz,
pass a man selling bouquets of mint,
pyramids of olives, their black glitter
oiled in sunlight. As I walk north
the tower of Suleyman's mosque falls back,
my landmark; I can't read Arabic, so that's
how I find the right shop, a black marble
arch incised in a necklace of gilt letters.
I climb chunks of stone stolen from a ruin;
Aziz leans over my hand, threatening to kiss it.
Two of his shop boys sort disks of agate.

In one corner, a thousand strings:
trade beads stratas' of color, pressed clay,
lapis, opaque glass, pinned or hooked
to the walls, cases housing six inch daggers,
Siwa silver collars, Beduoin face masks,
their worn fabrics sewn with coins, cowie
shells, carnelian. Trunks cover the floor, filled
with silver. I sift through earrings press-cut
with the name of Allah. Aziz hides his old
Nubian gold, his Venetian beads.
After five years of coming here he
can afford to tease me, call me Morticia
for the look I give him, when he bends over
my wrist, in a city where touch is a crime.

Before I buy tomb-looted scarabs,
he shows me pictures, small men with sidelocks,
in skullcaps, wearing hand-sewn clothes.
Until this century the Jews of Yemen refused
to teach the Arab tribes to sand cast, even
hammer silver to sheath their hooked daggers.

Aziz teaches me to look at the resolution
of the beading, tells me about the guild
El Toggar, the shahabander, their leader.
For centuries camels trolled the sand from Yemen
to Arabia, packing the guild's silver.
Aziz admires their craft, although
there are no more Jews in Cairo.

His hands animate, he describes coins
found in a tunnel in Fayuum oasis.
He took them out of town in a false bottom
he'd soldered on a gas can. The whole village,
a clan, was in on the con. They'd come
to Al Muezz, found his shop, shown him
three gold coins, Graeco-Roman. Back in Cairo,
disinterred from the gas can, the rest,
for which he'd paid a hundred thousand dollars,
in their acid bath, turned not gold, but black.

Golden Moon Casino

In the tub, bubbles sparkle and hiss.
I sniff orange and neroli, turn my body
that warms like a baby. On this hard mattress,
buttoned into pockets, I once cut powder lines.
The floor's blue ground floats yellow circles.
Gold drapes expose the fish tank of the parking lot.
A window seat narrows, made for robots,
tilts forward as if the whole room could lift.
Curtains pierced like shower liners rattle
across a porthole onto Alabama pines.

My family jams circles into slot machines.
Oz is here, drawing his curtains. I laid my head
on my Mama's stomach: "I want you to die
in my arms." "Then I'll wait for you," she said.
On the phone I told her I loved her, said
"I'm coming back early." She broke
two syllables, "You are?" into a question.
The words rose, opened like a bubble,
planetary, a circle in which she knew
that "o" in the word *love* was meant for her.

Pilgrim

When Amira's mother cooked *molucheyyah*,
she offered it to Hamid, camped under
the basement stairs, his steps ripe with refuse.
Seven times she made the hajj to Mecca,

so we called her Hagga Sab'a. Hair in a snood,
before first light, at 4:00, she bent towards
an open Koran on a stool she'd set before her,
a cloth draped over her head, lips following the Arabic.

When Hagga Sab'a penciled accounts in a notebook,
gold links winked from her neck; hoops crimped her ears.
A hundred *Fellaheen* families tended her cotton,
her apricots, near Sohag, Minya, Akhmim.

Hagga Sab'a picked each leaf off mint,
dried for tea on newsprint. Our food sat all day
after she'd cooked it: eggplant in oil, lentil soup
with tiny limes beside it, bread painted in egg yolk.

On her sideboard was a carton the size of a dress
box from my childhood, full of anise, cinnamon,
lemon biscuits. Family or friends called each night
at eleven, drank their tea in glass cups stuffed with mint.

They waved the flies away, opened newspapers
as placemats on clear plastic that covered a silk
cloth embroidered in Syria, while Zouzou prayed
at the end of the table. Zouzou, her oldest, is a dentist,

and epileptic from marriages of cousins.
Before I slept, three Koran under the mattress
beneath, Zouzou stuck a heart that read
I love you, in English script, to the bedstead.

A History in Valentines

The paper is pin-pricked, so the river, the canoe, the wilderness fold into
        the
envelope. Cars printed with *Car—ing for you,* scattered with glitter, stop
at red, green & lemon lights. Little bear still plays a record of silver
glitter, needle stuck in a black vinyl scratch, (the place my
father's hands lie folded in his coffin). The 70's clown, a
balloon bouquet in his gloved clutch, with yellow afro:
(the night I slept with the guy whose wrist bracelets
chafed). My mother's vacancy, (spent air
in a heart shape). Pocohontas' black braids
rest on her shoulder, while the boy in a
coonskin cap (like my brother's kept in
a drawer long after), steers his canoe
down a foldable river.

Guns Not For Sale

In the pawn shop cases, gold bands are snuck
into black velvet slits. Little beds of loss,
seeded under windexed glass, blue water
drops, a benediction. A sign reads *License
Being Renewed.* My first husband gave me
a forty-five, nickel-plated; I hit the target's
eye the first try. The store carries scooters,
motorcycles, chainsaws. Mylar balloons
bounce like silver heads. The stiff-haired
blonde is cordial; she gets to wear the cocktail
rings. Her linoleum is buffed; in the shop
window pennants flicker their tongues.
Outside, the paint is chipped, exposed wood
warps the roof line; a brimming camellia
outsmarts the neighborhood. Each flower tells
its story, each bud an explosive promise set
in glossed leaves, open-palmed, pink badges,
flat-faced ladies, yellow tasseled, desire spent.

Souvenir

She stands two inches high, her crooked table
lurches on china pilasters.
                    The transfer
of script reads, "Oysters, Sir?"
                          She sells
two rolls, a latticed pie, two lobsters painted
red-orange, the rise of their backs molded in china.

I keep paper clips in her barrel, empty of oysters.

You know she'd say *Kind Sir*; you know her eyes,
tiny almonds with heavy lashes, a flower of a mouth—
her name would be Pearl—is made to open.

She has to sell herself or she'll starve.

In the doctor's office, a false Grandfather clock.

Inside it a gong: a huge brass pan one could fry
oysters in.
                In a gladiator movie someone would slam
it with a mallet.
                    Ships would sail for Troy.

After the dilation drops the doctor put his microscope
right up against my eye.

                        I looked into the bulb of light.

It's only a floater. He pointed to the globe of the eye,
told me: *It's not a retinal tear* (as if the window shade
had not pulled away), *only the shrinking of the vitreous fluid.*

I hear what she hears, time's hiss, holding the shell to her ear.

Float

The hippo gathers water
around herself drawing
her cloak down,
sinks and leaves
a siphoning circle
water draining downward.
That's what stars are,
holes hippos leave
diving through night.
Tiny ears and eyes ride
up as she surfaces, breathes, tunnels again
in slow circles, in her small pool;
she drags night
itself a circle of swimming,
as time is a curtain
of shifts, elastic.
In the act of seeing,
I am never beside a loss but within
a wisteria as it works drapery into the woods.
I hear bells on the high-heeled wood
shoes of the Florentine whores.

The Turkomen Brothers

In this apartment near
the Bosphorus,
where under the moon's
dagger *Natashas*
from the Balkans
swarm the courtyard,
we sit on the floor,
first against wall
cushions, then closer
in to the tablecloth.
We meet wives
with heads in kerchiefs,
Russian doll sets
of sons, a girl's
cheeks sewn with her father's
sand-fly-bites.
A toddler son wades in,
topples a tower
of Fanta into lamb
& stewed eggplant.
Tribes are selling
their treasures:
fire-gilded, etched silver,
chest pieces
like huge plates,
high headdresses
for women that sit
like armor, whips
with carnelian-studded
handles, made
by people called
Mongols, who spun
the swords stored
above the ladder in their shop.

Ahmad once tried
to tell me their story,
in English so broken,
it was like trying to read
a scatter of pebbles,
or coffee silt in our cups.
First Russians came,
then their land
went back to Afghanistan.
He and *older brother*
trudged across mountains,
crossed on foot
all of Iran and Turkey,
sold dung, picked fruit,
found other Ersari here,
opened shops
under the bazaar's domed
roofs, bricked in spirals
made before
Columbus was born.
I've bought from him
a chair that sits four inches
off the ground,
its back carved wood,
its seat woven sinew,
a chest piece whose carnelians
glow like burnt tribal eyes.
In three years
he'll call me in Tennessee
to ask for a letter
to come to America.
He'll forget to leave
the name of a Turkish official,
an address. There are
no yurts outside New York.

Refuge

Most of what we see in Tennessee
are ruby-throated. The color of a red
lollypop, globes hold sugar water
where hummingbirds feed their way south.
Even butterflies are nomadic. Driven
through Mexico, car wheels slip
through a crush of monarchs. In Brazil, people step
on wafers, morpho everywhere. Wings thin
as paper prayers, so many crowd the flowering
trees they crack the branches. Above
the forest's canopy, blue males float.
Thousands of wings blink, metallic, so pilots,
in flight, see their blue silk.

Above the Mississippi, a cloud cliff,
its pink a high iceberg, hangs, a turning
pedestal to light. A pair of orange
monarchs fly attached. Their bodies are spindles
that touch; one fits its wings inside the other's.
I creep up where they land, pulsing together.
A pressing slides between them, a fluid
like tears or the sticky nub of lily stigma,
petals flecked black, stamens shivering pollen.

Visiting from Bhutan, two monks plan
to throw the sand from their mandala
into the river. They map the Buddhist
universe. Sands in jars heighten to fuchsia,
goldenrod, egg blue. The lamas sit close,
as if playing chess, holding long tubes, tapping
along a metal cap, the kind pastry chefs use,
so a dribble of sand, thin as the vein in an hourglass,
an ink of grains, spills. Together
they edge a fluted border like a doily.

Watered grass green orders the border's
orange and yellow petals. Inside:
drizzled clouds, prayer wheels, tiny shells.

The monks have left time's bridge—
that raining in the hourglass. Attachment.
But I beat my heart on stones, a river
running over. In this world, a garter snake,
thin yellow ribbons moving in its back,
pulls into its mouth the hind leg of a immobile
toad. I stoop to watch. The snake disgorges;
the toad hops forward. From his leg
two sores ooze—like my skinned knee as a kid
where my mother painted a mercurochrome
rabbit. A yellowjacket lights
at the blood the mouth has left.

Zabiba

Yellowed skin sacks, bones rolling inside them—
an apparition of camels, driven from Libya.
On her curb, her overscarf black, underscarf
tight on her forehead, she squats over coals.
She's bound chicken feathers to make a fan.
Corn ears blacken. *Allah u Akbar*—recorded,
a man's voice floats, speakers wired high up
in the mosque's turrets. Pink light blinks
in the waves of the Nile. Turkeys, daubed
with red growths, cough near the water man.
In his closet of a shop he sifts coins back
into my hand. He's banged a prayer bruise
into his forehead, touched it to the ground
over and over. Like cantaloupes' sweet navels.

Lipoma

On the internet it looked like a plum
pulled from its skin, ripped whole;
the pit held all pulp around it, slipping
its peel. The surgeon drew mine: a spider,
or chrysanthemum; its petals siphoned out,
a nubbed starfish clamped in. He shaded
between the arms & said, *I could hardly tell*
the healthy tissue. Then my arm was swollen,
the dug-out part numb, a soft avocado.
His father was a surgeon. And taxidermist,
he cut small cadavers open, like ones posted
on shelves in catfish restaurants near Shiloh.
Coons, squirrel, an old bobcat's frayed ear tufts,
various glass-eyed racks. He's hung duck-hunting
posters. Things grow inside, replicate, take shapes:
daddy long legs stroking in, or petals build like
fishscales, tender as oyster. The vessel
of netting clots with artifact, metaphors.

The Reading Room Deck

He took out three girls who roomed
together; she got the short straw
& married him. The foam crochets
itself over and over while the ocean
undoes itself to put its body on the beach.
John Jacob Astor, the words, released
in conversation, ribbon in the wind.
Rockweed's mustard & black laces spin
and drift, leashed to granite flatbeds.
Withdrawing water tamps itself into sand,
gravity draws down, the word *settlement*
skeined and yanked like salt water taffy
gliding in orbit on the arms of the pull machine.
Below, stays clink against masts; a dozen
gulls kite and fall. A wood porch hangs
over the beach; a waitress in a white
uniform brings her chowder, oyster
crackers, butter balls. *My great aunt slept*
with her stepfather is her unspoken sentence.
A lobsterman churns in from his day; others
attend their salads. The red nun bangs
in his cut silk wake, lemon on her fingers.

In This Neighborhood

It wasn't Carlton Gary, dapper, teeth
white & even, but black-skinned,
who bit and strangled seven old women.
But someone's son, who spilled a bloody
Mary on his madras shorts at the club,
whose crooked teeth crowded his mouth
when he smiled to apologize.

He was the guy who jogged at night.
The bite impression was never introduced
at trial, was kept from the defense.
June brings the swelter, but wafts
cinnamon magnolia, gardenia's sugars.
Through pines, woodpeckers drag their reds.
Lawns, plush with fescue, hum with sprinklers.

Carlton summers on death row. Questions
bubble. DA, defense, Judge, drove their convertibles
to the clubhouse by the river. Hedges are shaped,
clipped. The real killer's grandmother smelled
of powder; lipstick ran spider legs around her mouth.
One bloodied woman was left, the coroner
let slip, with a pinecone tucked inside her.

The Strangler's Neighborhood

A barbell, a tomahawk, scattered camels glint
in the squares of the charms' tray;
a woman with a buzz cut watches as I survey
the flattened gold chains, men's Vegas rings,
big enough to rake a cheek. Scores of pearl
necklaces laid neatly recall the woman in
Dinglewood Pharmacy who spooned bun,
then hotdog, chili, oyster crackers, and pickles,
salted and peppered. She'd swiveled carefully
on the turquoise vinyl of her stool,
checkered linoleum mirrored in metal.
She would have left at the pawn her husband's
golf clubs, a son's guitar. A milkshake
burned sweet cold in the back of her throat.

Hour of the Cardinals

A judge from Tupelo tells me tankers
piss dioxin past the shotgun shacks.
Done eat the asphalt white.
'Drive til it's empty' is what they told.

Sparrows come through portals
in the fence's chain link windows. Colic
means *inconsolable*, my sister tells me.
The Pope knew about the gassing of the Jews.

He turned like an eggplant when he died,
all black. In my dining room, a horse
comes through the wall, charcoal scratched
on the surface of white-washed feed sacks.

At five, in the winter, they come
six or seven, red-feathered in the boxwood,
for sunflower seeds, a heat's compression
soaked into the cobbled face of a flower.

Abuse travels inside like the shadow of a ricochet.
Lawanda left with her girlfriend
for one of the Carolinas. She emailed
to tell me she'd seen the sea.

Novitiate

Christ on his cross floats sideways in the air
like the wooden T of a puppeteer.

From his feet, hands, and rib, strings of blood
drip into a monk puppet's twin stigmata.

The monk's tonsured head tips up, as if
to catch snowflakes on his tongue.

Centuries later, the air conditioner turns over.
But who would want that—to be tied

hand and foot? Recorded inside:
our mothers' voices, caustic or kind,

caught in the wheels of our small minds.
So many candles lit for Mary.

The practice of belief is like learning to form
first the alphabet, then words.

San Bernardino's dark, vast as a dancehall,
foams voices that stream and disappear.

Who wouldn't want a pink heaven
built like Siena, air scored by rosemary's

needles, vistas of grape vines knitting,
palazzo shadows black as licorice.

I read names above buzzers: Bartolo,
Giovanni, Fiorenzani. Someone sneezes

behind shutters. An old woman I might become
clatters dishes, scolds her daughters.

Under hoods of glass, icy vats of hazelnut,
pistachio, chocolate gelato, are scooped into

sweet communion I take from a waxed cup.
My mother greeted yet another hospice priest

with his kit of wafers and chalice. I exited;
I'd had communion three times that week.

After chemo she stood before the mirror;
her hands covered her hair and I laid

my own behind hers, so she could see how
a tonsured head would look. I sat beside

while she slept. She'd open her eyes, gaze
spooled into mine: her blue wonder.

IV

Launch

I

Water lands its warmth in my hands
as I soap and sponge the small
50's glass; its heavy bottom weights
my palm. Two red-orange antelope,
rampant, leap trees in a chase
as my hands turn the glass.

Through the window, four cardinals,
loosed chips in a kaleidoscope, whirl
into the redbud, then still, clipped
to the branches like ornaments.
The males turn their masks of black
fire, the faces of Chinese Nuo dancers.

I turn my spy glass; they launch
a game of branch to branch. Bright
notes each moment, red and black,
they flurry up the scale and back,
lavender redbud to tufted gingko and back.
Then they have flown like antelope.

2

I heard the knocker, the thud of its fall,
then banging with a fist, next thing
he was upstairs, a floral maze in polyester
against his chest, dark hair, something
about "checking the electric." I held my breath
behind the dried-clay face mask that
saved me. Then he thundered back down
the red carpet. I slammed the front door,
turned a brass ram's head to bolt it,
wandered into the living room where someone
had yanked drawers open. My mother
hadn't bothered with the lock. The cop
told her I was lucky. I turned
page after page of mug shots.

3

I had a job, insurance, could say
"I am *this*"or "I am *that,*"
but outside the window birds,
jacketed in blues and blacks, glistened
in sunlight, flew and flew back.

4

Your hand here, the nurse said, *but don't grasp,*
just rest your arm. She cupped my breast
in her palm, then laid it on the cold shelf.
It flattened as the upper plate slid down.
Sandwiched between panes of glass,
flesh caught, I couldn't move.

Don't breathe, she said; birds flew
the wallpaper's border. In Tibet I bought
a small rug. Ribbons of cloud
wind through a prayer wheel that spins
its prayers out. I shook each weaver's
hand, saying *Tashidelai* all around the atelier.

5

Sandy's cat dragged a bird
to her yard. Sleek, black, rubbed
in purple dust. A grackle. It tilted lopsided
and flapped. She filled up a bucket.
It was warm in my hands, didn't struggle.

6

Using repetitive steps in a pattern
Nuo dancers fend off the dark with gongs,
tilt their heads behind their masks
when the rice tassels. They fear
failed harvests, siblings who kill.
They juggle burning stones, swallow
fire. Two thousand years of dancing
and we want to slam ourselves into traffic.
The way a bird is slapped by the window
it flies into.

7

A sparrow tilts and catches
for a perch at the bars on my window.
Head fluffy, it fins its tail, balancing,
feathers not quite long enough, learning to steer.
Weightlessness following.

Sparrows' Vision

Tiny ones are pecked with a dense freckling,
pin dot browns like the point of a fountain
pen. Inside, a cream, so the pattern shows
on the screen of what the tiny sparrow might see
before the splash of light and shadow.
Red salvia's torches, globes of red sugar-
water call a hummingbird's spinning.

A chittering—a tiny green skiff shoots
through air, small as okra, dips its needle
in the well of a plastic flower.
I learn the redbird's call: three long, five quick.
Lined with a paper membrane, the robin's
shell spits paint chips, a Tiffany
blue I want to line a hallway in my mind.

Like a mind it breaks under the tiniest
effort. Into a cradle of pain spring floats
another baby, hatching complications
in her brain. When a jay douses a sparrow in stabs,
a score of sparrows edge in, shuffle, fan
like curtains of heat,
helpless as seraphim and cherubim.

On the walls of Hagia Sophia such angels
glitter into mosaic, gold, brown, red
chips set—portraits of Michael and Gabriel
who must shake their heads over us.
We can't interpret the birds,
or shake meaning from each other's speech,
as we fly at the windows of each others' lives.

The Raggle Taggle Gypsies

Her chalk notes, a Braille I never understood.

On the page, five parallel lines: a fence
or strung wires, ink-tailed drops of black;
where did the birds live?

                    The record disks
spat static. The school was an old mansion
with a domed ballroom.

                    The music room's
forbidden balcony overlooked, through French doors,
the old drive. Spiked iron gates, tipped gold,
led through high pines, the track a bed
of needles.

                    Her belt tight, as if pregnant,
hair greased grey, Mrs. Parla played through rumors:
her six children sardines, some tiny apartment.

We each held a music textbook, hard covers,
with sharp points. Illustrations wreathed each
ballad.

                    A castle, a Lord, gypsies, the Lady
who ran away. They say the Lady was the sixth
Earl's wife, Jean, of Cassilis, the gypsy, Johnny Faa.

They hanged him, sealed her in a stone tower.

I could hear the song, but not follow the black
spots, drops of notes, little anchors, sailing
like Sir Patrick Spens.

I did find him, the man
illustrated in my head.

Mrs. Parla when
she lay beside her blind husband, had
music's threads a bird would steal into a nest.

Before the Prophet's Birthday

Stars threaded into a fragrant necklace,
a string of jasmine swings from the cab's
rear view mirror. The driver has painted white
letters in Arabic along the black wheel,
so his fingers turn the words of Allah.

Along the Corniche banyan trees, trunks
woven like ropes, shade the young girls'
oval faces, framed in head scarves;
sweet eyes darken as the boys flock.
Bells ripple under a horse's throat.

Sheep, long pink stripes down their backs,
trundle to a stop. I've come to shop
for nougat, sheets of nuts in hardened syrup,
sugar dolls to celebrate the prophet. I'm *infidel*
so a Beduoin, tattooed line down her chin, hisses.

Stuffed hedgehogs and mink climb the walls
of the spice shop. Moths powder the bins
of hibiscus tea, beside burlap sacks of henna's
green flour. Over the scale's compass
drying on glass: a bloody handprint.

A chain-maker's store has no front;
it's a soot-covered shack. Bare-handed,
he holds a link; his red-hot pincers squeeze
its ends together. Inside is oven-black.
Hubcaps hang from a flame tree on the sidewalk.

A stairway of colored lights strung
up the flame tree, apple smoke curls
from shishas; I tuck a bill in his filthy pocket

as a boy sleeps against his sister and brother
like puppies laid over each other.

"Bukra fil mish mish," people say:
the fortnight the apricots ripen, or
when the apricots come, meaning
"once in a blue moon."
A flood in the heart.

Tectonic

The whorl inside we call cat's eyes,
vertigo spun inside a common marble.

As if the sidewalk shifts, the way
an escalator propels us from under.

A tilting, like ice breaks boys would ride
down the Hudson, crust splitting
against itself like a puzzle's wood edges.

Slid back together, its flattened
frogs made a comprehensible world
on a pull-down classroom map.

Black letters followed curves of rivers,
spelling Indus, Mississippi.
                              Washington
crossed the Delaware, his myth heroic
in a boat, nibbled with ice floes.

In the Kalahari lions owned a time of day
to drink, each species safe
in a Noah's ark of assent.

                    The rest of us
already footage, the planet a small marble,
its fires burn the dark.

                    The Dalai Lama's
trail from Tibet a filament of blue drizzle
like sifted magnetic dust on an etch-a-sketch.

A narrative like a piece of music, notated
in a language of black birds not everyone
can read.

            Hammer-headed, red-caps,
they wing it, sliding into the next tree
like home plate, with a folding of wings,
umbrellas of black.

                    Someday their woods
will be under glass.

Inside lego sets of cities, computers will seed
and reap, where tomatoes once ripened under real
sun.

        Someone will own a greenhouse
with the last pileated.

                    Smells lost: air run
over the backs of deer, oiled rank by bear.

This late in the day a cardinal snapped to a branch,
snow, sun a halo, tilts something inside us.

The Ecology of *Atlas*

Head-dressed in orange down, the color of Georgia,
he wears two white mantles; his feelers splay,
two minnows' fishbones, delicate as lashes.

He
holds his nine inch spread on four furred nubs
palmed to a leaf, his rear legs tucked under
its edge.

Four white patches arrest us, the whole
embroidery complex as a Chinese robe, silked
in oranges, whites and greys.

Even his segmented
carapace is eyed on its underside, no part of his
body is not marked.

Under a microscope
his whole cape is mailed with shining platelets,
a roman army's phalanx glinting their shields so sun
becomes a weapon.

Seeing him soaking through his colors
is to learn regard of a small god.

*

Inside this domed
atrium, steaming with released humidity, in the eighty
degrees butterflies like, morphos glint silver, polished
to blue; swallowtails flash emerald glitter.

Small Postmen
deliver their reds.

On the undersides of seeded fern,
Paper Kites, a dozen black and white sails hung
upside-down, each in a luff, inflate.

Pale yellow
Sulphers make a circlet of flutter around and around
each other, drawing wreaths in the air that show
and disappear.

Like Tinkerbell, her wand sparking,
they trail pollen, attach themselves one frill to another,
thrift to butterfly bush to bee balm to sedum, they
soak the cosmos.

So this *Atlas* in his brown study
holds on.

Each *Atlas*, winged, beating, holds up invisible
circles that link us to each other, lands on us without fear.

At the Piano

Love is the wind that hurries through all
our lives and like the leaves spins, bastes the sky
blue. The sax player is careful with my eardrums.
My husband stabs at the keys and roils them
into sound, tilts his head, sways over the long steps
of black and white. Into this room leaks the
honey of late sun.   His blues fog the mountains;
in their dips balance the late day's tea cups.

Ruler

A pink ruler bent
upright at one end like a ski,
her head lifted, as if in meditation, or in wait

for whoever comes
into her sea of copper leaves.
Her tail tapers, a wick lit through brocade, scales

woven into pattern
like botehs in a carpet. Boteh,
the shape of paisley, stylized bush, shrub, under

which she rides billows
of shadows. Pink gold presses through
as sun slides behind our mountain; leaves yellow,

redden, drizzle downward
into a shuffle. On the cattle farm's fence,
yellow and black, a two-inch spider whose forearms

shape a shovel, floats
inside her knitting. Water runs its scales
under grass so thick even the culvert's invisible.

A blue mouse spits
through grass. A cow and her calf
break upward, scuttle from their wallow. Into

the stillness cows make
come whirls of birds; turning, their
undersides go white, then black, tear upward,

settle into spaces between
cows and spout forward. They blow
into sun. I cannot look into their coming and going,

ghost shape, boteh spun
from starlings. A bright surprise like
the step onto its wand, one's death, its pink measure.

Morphic Fields

A sheet of sparrows breaks; each bobs
for seed. Sheldrake tells us why they move
as one. Bird calls hang in trees, cheeps,
a toss of pitches. A cardinal's red dash through
winter's grey nets. My friend wanted to knit,
like the swan girl, green nettles' thread into
sweaters, to turn her brothers from swans
into men again. Their beaks carried her,
suspended in a net hammock, over the sea.
A king found her; she kept silent to keep
her brothers alive. The gunsmith's hound spends
hot days on a tarp, slung for shade in his pen;
today he's warm inside their trailer. In the trailer
park white monopoly-block houses flock.
Cows in the fields, like plastic miniatures,
honk and low. Horses' heads dip, rhythmic
as they walk, draped in blue blankets. Spools
of hay fit nooks in the red barn. In the end
it's always the stepmother. Sheldrake's tricked
the tax man. You can't call it a yard if twin
angus wander; now it's part of the farm. With
two cows who can argue? The seven swans
wore crowns, though, as they flew her through
the dark. Her real stepmother never wore
clothes. And her own mother never left the
household of eleven. Nettles tore her fingers;
perhaps they bled to stain all cardinals red.

Little Lost Girls

1

This green plastic barrette belongs in a case
with cylinder seals one rolled into clay at Sumer,
chlorite or ivory cut with wheat, trees, a priestess.
It's the brightest of grasses, luminous, as if dipped
in some iridescent finish reminiscent of fish.

Its four six-petaled flowers, two leaves,
overflow a wheeled barrow like a bassinet.
Two tiny wheels have eight spokes each, a shape
old as Mesopotamia. The wheel's innovations
didn't change until pneumatic tires.

These green forget-me-nots, a shape
worked in every carpet woven, this
battle cart, chariot, car is a tiny
symbol for civilization, as we lose our
handhold on the planet, once a fertile crescent.

2

A professor of religion sends me
barrettes she finds in cinders, nestled
on cigarette butts & silken dirt. They
collect on my desk: white bow, red butterfly,
pink hippo in a dress, plastic, ever-lasting.

In the fairy tale, the priestess anoints
me with beauty forever; she rolls time
back, or forward and I am twenty. The whole
kingdom freshens, lit after rain, pushing energy up
so watermelons, peppers, tomatoes bulge & glisten.

I walk on woven carpets, soft as a lamb just
washed. I am not overturned, cut open, sliced
from inside, trying to put my own guts
back in my stomach. I was never erased,
betrayed, never wanted to walk into traffic.

3

The carriage rolls on and I cannot stop
its coursing. Now a cindered track
unfurls ahead through pine, hickory,
sweet gum, trunks straight, no underbrush;
a bent creek plays its waters.

The mountains are so dense with rock,
they cannot be civilized, turned under the trees
violent press of green. In our minds the earth
absorbs itself, vortexes draw us in like nets,
spin us in webs of fears we've manifested.

My judgment, envy, evaporates
in the circle of minds we make,
a ring of higher selves, pulling something
good, we call it wishes, our earnest certainty,
out of the absence of ego, clipped to belief.

Notes

"Blue Rose"

Sheila Jordan (born Sheila Jeanette Dawson, November 18th, 1928) is an American jazz singer and songwriter. She pioneered a bebop and scat jazz singing style with an upright bass as the only accompaniment. Scott Yanow described her as "one of the most consistently creative of all jazz singers," and Charlie Parker often introduced her as "the singer with the million dollar ears."

"Blue Fawn"

Clarence "Herb" Robertson (born February 21, 1951) is a jazz trumpeter and flugelhornist. He has recorded five solo albums for the JMT record label and worked as a sideman for Tim Berne, Anthony Davis, Bobby Previte, David Sanborn, George Gruntz, Bill Frisell and Paul Motian. (He plays with the Fonda/Stevens Group, one of my husband's bands.)

"Henry Darger Comes to Lakebottom Park"
& other Darger Poems I–VIII

Henry Joseph Darger, Jr. (born April 12, 1892–April 13, 1973) was an outsider artist and writer who worked as a hospital custodian in Chicago, Illinois. He has become famous for an over 15,000 page manuscript entitled *The Story of the Vivian Girls, in What is Known as the Realms of the Unreal, of the Glandeco-Angelinian War Storm, Caused by the Child Slave Rebellion.* Several hundred drawings and watercolor paintings illustrate the story.

"Morphic Fields"

Rupert Sheldrake, a biologist and author, is best known for his hypothesis of morphic fields and morphic resonance, which leads to a vision of a living, developing universe with its own inherent memory. He worked in developmental biology at Cambridge University, where he was a Fellow of Clare College.

—Michael Stevens

Tina Barr's volumes of poetry include her first book, *The Gathering Eye,* winner of the Tupelo Press Editor's Award, *At Dusk on Naskeag Point, The Fugitive Eye,* and *Red Land, Black Land,* all winners of national chapbook competitions. She has received fellowships from the National Endowment for the Arts, the Tennessee Arts Commission, the Pennsylvania Council on the Arts, The MacDowell Colony, Virginia Center for the Creative Arts, and Ucross Foundation. Former director of the Creative Writing Program at Rhodes College and Charles R. Glover Chair of English Studies, she teaches in the Great Smokies Writing Program at UNCA.

CPSIA information can be obtained at www.ICGtesting.com
Printed in the USA
LVOW06s2339220315

431557LV00007B/9/P